Words That Stick

229 Simple Ideas To Help You Write Better
(Almost) Instantly

Newly Revised Edition

Rix Quinn

"Words That Stick- 229 Simple Ideas To Help You Write Better (Almost) Instantly," by Rix Quinn. ISBN 978-1-60264-873-9.

Published 2011 by Virtualbookworm.com Publishing Inc., P.O. Box 9949, College Station, TX 77842, US. ©2011, Rix Quinn. All rights reserved. No part of this publication may be reproduced, stored in a retrieval system, or transmitted in any form or by any means, electronic, mechanical, recording or otherwise, without the prior written permission of Rix Quinn.
Manufactured in the United States of America

Contents

This book is lovingly dedicated to:
Erica Quinn, a wonderful wife and friend,
a former English teacher who knows worlds more
about vocabulary than her husband does.
Katie Quinn Fultz, a lovely, delightful daughter
and brilliant scholar, who teaches her middle-
aged dad something new every day.
Bill Quinn, a great father, superb author,
and outstanding role model.
Lennie Quinn, a terrific, loving mother and
former elementary school teacher who
introduced me to the written word.

Introduction
If you hate to write, this book is for you.

Right up front, I'm going to admit three things:

1. I was a semi-lousy student, but learning how to write saved my academic life.

2. A lot of people say writing is hard. No. Writing is easy. Singing a solo when you've forgotten the words is hard.

3. Writing should be simple, like choosing a meal at a fast food restaurant. In fact, think of *Words That Stick* as a menu that simplifies your life.
   Read the menu, choose what you need from each part of it, and pay no attention to the rest. Then, next time you need to write something, "dine" with us again.

Here's what you'll find on these few pages:

= Who is your primary reader? Find her in Chapter 1.

= What special styles can we learn from top word wizards? Check Chapter 3.

= Want to write better (almost) instantly? Then quickly turn to Chapter 4.

= Need an essay title or heading? Turn to Chapter 8 for 51 ideas.

= Want to grab your reader in the first paragraph and hold him throughout your paper? Then you should turn to Chapter 9 to find 60 techniques.

= The time when most readers flee is during those middle paragraphs. Better try the "declare and prepare" method we describe in Chapter 10.

= Want a fantastic finish for your short masterpiece? You'll find 30 outstanding conclusion ideas in Chapter 11.

This book is simple stuff. It's not loaded with fancy words or flowery phrases. *Words That Stick* simply wants to help you get inside your reader's mind and plant your idea in a positive, memorable way.

Come on. Give it a try. Next time you're hungry for theme ideas—or just need some fast food for thought—we want you to refer to us.

-- Rix Quinn, 2011

1
Who will read your writing?

It's the start of a new semester, and student council elections approach. A friend just nominated you for vice president. In three weeks, you've got to convince the entire school—including many who don't know you—why voting for you makes sense.

What do you say to convince them?

Or, if you're at work...

This morning your boss approached you and said, "Bob, at the national sales meeting next week, can you make a two-minute speech telling how you improved our distribution?"

Wow, you've got to sum up a year's work in 250 words, and also remind your boss your name's not Bob! Where do you go for help?

Here are a few ideas, and believe me, they're not rocket science. I'm no scientist, and I can prove that with my lousy math grades!

Anyway, first you must attract a crowd or readers. After that, you must keep them entertained long enough to implant ideas in their brains. In order to do that, you must know who you are speaking to.

How to think about your audience/readers

A public speaker remarked that when he drafts his speech, he pictures a single composite person, the typical individual he'll be talking to. In order to define that person, he'll need to know:

1. *Age*. Will he be talking to senior citizens, or high school seniors?

2. *Gender*. Is he addressing a men's, a women's, or a mixed group?

3. *Ethnicity*. Is he speaking to an ethnically diverse group or is the audience predominantly black, white, latino, asian, native american? Is the ethnicity of the group the same as that of the speaker/author?

4. *Education*. Has the audience attended high school, college, graduate school?

5. *Economic status*. Is the crowd rich, poor, middle class, executives, laborers, self-made?

6. *Cultural background*. Is the group working class, intellectual, urban sophisticates, country plain, old-school refined, brash upstarts, new-age spiritualists, traditional, vegetarian, steak-and-potatoes?

7. *Political beliefs*. Are they conservative, liberal, moderate, anarchists, or a mixture of political beliefs?

8. *Degree of familiarity*. Is he addressing friends and family, seldom-seen relatives, business

2

colleagues, complete strangers, or some combination of familiar and unfamiliar individuals?

9. *Peers, subordinates, or superiors*. Is he speaking to a group of equals, or are they his bosses or employees?

10. *Expertise*. Does his audience already know a lot about his topic? Can he assume familiarity with concepts, terms of art, and acronyms?

11. *Audience aims*. In addition, he might ask himself why his audience would be interested in what he has to say. What is their agenda? Most important, what can he tell them that they've never heard before?

2
General rules for approaching your audience/readers

Be sensitive to ethnicity, gender, disability.

Ask yourself if you really need to label an individual ethnically. It's usually not necessary. If you don't need to, don't do it.

If you must describe an individual's ethnicity, be specific about country of origin. For example, Japanese-American, Taiwanese-American, or Korean-American are preferable to Asian; Mexican-American, Costa Rican–American, Honduran-American to Latino.

When country of origin is unknown, terms like black, African-American, Asian, Latino, in the right context, can be appropriate. (If you're speaking or writing to a specific group, it might be a good idea to ask the organization's director or president how the group would like to be addressed.)

To avoid the perception of gender bias, use masculine and feminine pronouns equally, alternating he and she, his and hers, him and her. This is preferable to she/he and other awkward gender-neutral uses of pronouns.

Be aware of the prevailing terms. For example: "actor" is now used in some circumstances to describe both male and female performers.

Avoid traps of familiarity.

Not long ago, I e-mailed my daughter at college, beginning the letter "Hi, honey," and signing it "I love you." I accidentally mailed it to a new client, who did not appreciate me calling him "honey."

Keep correspondence focused, straightforward, and proper... and make sure you apply the right address.

Be careful when using humor.

A teacher or boss may not appreciate insensitive jokes.

Keep word choices simple.

Choosing a complicated word when a simpler one works just as well might be considered showing off. Most readers, no matter how well educated, prefer simple, direct language. For example, why use "prevaricate" when "lie" will do?

Two critical issues

Today's writer must get to the point quickly, reinforce opinions with facts, and stick to one single subject. Otherwise, that writer risks losing the reader.

Sad but true: Today's writer must also amuse the reader while she informs him. That's the most important idea in this book. And we'll show you all sorts of techniques to make your work more powerful, engaging, and—most important—memorable.

How to develop shrinking thinking

Way, way back in the early 1960s, the auto industry manufactured long, roomy, luxurious passenger cars.

> *America's first victim of vicious verb virus was William Henry Harrison. Ole Tippacanoe. You've heard of him, right? The former president?*
>
> *Remember what he did in office? Mainly, he just died. When he got elected in 1840, he crafted a real tonsil-buster of a speech...three hours and who knows how many pages long.*
>
> *Lousy idea. He delivered it on a gloomy, rainy day, without an overcoat. He got chilled and caught a cold. That cold turned into pneumonia. Then he took a turn for the worse. Then he took a turn into the cemetery. And that's how he became an ex-president.*
>
> *The lesson: Shorter speeches may be better for your health!*

Then a remarkable print advertisement from Volkswagen turned people's perceptions upside down. On a huge page it showed a little VW Beetle in the distance. The headline said, "Think small."

Throughout this text, we'll be shrinking, shrinking, shrinking. Each time you come upon new information, think about:

= Its value to your various audiences.

= The major point of the information.

= How you can present it in an exciting way. Will it require an anecdote, an example, a quote, or a comparison?

= How you can simplify it, so virtually anyone can grasp it.

= How you can present it in a way that makes it unforgettable.

3
Famous word wizards and their writing styles

Let's talk briefly about some amazing word wizards. Each created a systematic way to imprint messages on an audience. You may want to emulate one of their styles, or create your own.

Aesop
Around 600 b.c. this Greek slave began to chronicle fables from around the civilized world. He became so famous his master freed him, and he traveled many places to share stories with both kings and commoners.

His stories—like the one about the tortoise and the hare—gave animals human qualities. His fables pointed out people's good and bad traits and illustrated critical life lessons.

What a great idea, huh?

Aristophanes
Did you know somebody wrote comedy back in 400 b.c.? Too bad they didn't have television then, because this guy combined plays with song and rhythm that provided constant entertainment for ancient Greeks.

What skills about short writing do we learn from him?

(1) Teach with humor, and (2) employ rhythm and song as a memory device.

Socrates

He lived about the same time as Aristophanes. What we know of him comes from the writings of his star pupil, Plato. Socrates helped people seek ultimate truths by questioning conventional wisdom and examining their own beliefs.

He believed folks should not accept opinion as fact. Instead, they should search further for true meaning.

Sadly, his persistent questions riled public officials, who sentenced him to death by drinking hemlock.

And his last question, "Is this stuff poison?" was reluctantly answered, "Yep."

From Socrates we learn that questions are a powerful way to begin any form of writing. They arouse curiosity, which prompts people to read more.

Sophocles

Hey, did you notice everybody we've talked about so far has only one name? (Don't worry. We'll get to last names in just a minute.)

This author created plays that usually centered on a single heroic character who—in order to help humankind—chose an unpopular course of action.

Sophocles introduces us to (1) the popularity of contrarian thinking and (2) the value of building a story around a hero.

Benjamin Franklin

This famous American championed succinct writing, and his epigrams have become part of our cultural heritage. Ben warned, "He that speaks much is much mistaken," and "Here comes the orator, with his flood of words and his drop of reason."

Apprenticed as a printer's helper, Franklin studied the handbills and circulars his shop printed. When newsletters and newspapers began in the colonies, Franklin would submit letters or witty sayings under a pseudonym.

Each time he saw his work in print, he became more energized. And his creation Poor Richard's Almanac became a best-seller.

What attracted readers to him?

a. He wrote simply. Franklin knew his audience, and focused on basic words and ideas.

b. He wrote briefly. The almanac emphasizes frugality, humility, and brevity. "Silence is not always a sign of wisdom, but babbling is ever a mark of folly," Franklin said.

c. He wrote timelessly. Instead of addressing contemporary issues, Franklin wrote more about human traits, like this one on picking friends: "He that lies down with dogs shall rise up with fleas."

d. He spoke of moral truths. "Glass, china, and reputation are easily cracked and never well mended."

e. He used humor. Franklin's sayings are among the most quoted in history. We'd do well to fly Franklin's kite.

Mark Twain (Samuel L. Clemens)

He's been called America's finest author because he wrote in American dialect, using phrases and speech unique to the United States. In an age filled with serious, pompous prose, Twain laced his stories with regional references, offbeat characters, and comedy.

What else did he do to hold the reader?

a. Secondary sources. Twain claimed many of his stories came from others. In his first nationally acclaimed short story, "The Celebrated Jumping Frog of Calaveras County," Twain related a tale reportedly told to him over dinner.

This was almost a form of testimonial or validation by another person. His secondary sources gave the stories more impact.

b. Write from experience. Twain weaves his own life background into several stories. You can do the same thing, no matter what your age! Each of us offers a unique, valuable perspective on living.

In fact, Twain cites his early apprenticeship to a printer, and his later freelance writing for the Virginia City Nevada Enterprise, for providing him experience that later brought him fame.

"One isn't a printer ten years," Twain explained, "without setting up acres of good and bad literature, and learning—unconsciously at first, consciously later—to discriminate between the two, within his mental limitations; and meantime he is unconsciously acquiring what is called a 'style.'"

c. Life lessons. Twain's writings are often stories that teach a lesson. Most of us remember the one about Tom Sawyer, who concocts a plan to make a fence-painting chore so appealing his friends do the work for him.

The story is effective both as a narrative and as a lesson in human nature. It's about the effects of greed and sloth on individuals and the community.

d. Keep it simple. While scholars may examine Twain's writing on multiple levels, Twain knew that clarity was key. He used basic vocabulary and dialog to convey complex ideas.

Will Rogers

Superstar Will Rogers died in a 1935 plane crash, at the peak of his popularity. How many celebrities do you know who wrote a syndicated newspaper column, appeared on radio, headlined the theatrical circuit, and starred in movies?

Will rose to fame doing rope tricks, then began creating humorous one-liners. His comedy often emphasized topical and political humor.

Will skillfully turned current events into an effective opener to talk about other things. What current events are relevant to your academic or professional writing today?

The Generic Modern Politician

Forgive me for generalizing, but I've lumped all these folks into one giant category. You can recognize them by their blue suits, red ties, pancake makeup, and uncanny ability to sniff out any camera or microphone within three miles.

a. Like an exhibitionist, a candidate looks for exposure. But to get it, he must support an issue most people are for. (A majority of voters usually support better schools, more parades, and happy songs. They rarely favor higher taxes, lowered expectations, or local perverts.)

b. Many candidates zero in on a problem that needs to be solved. Then they offer a solution.

c. Some politicians link their ability to solve a current problem with past experience solving a similar problem.

d. Many office-seekers are masterful storytellers. For instance, they might discuss a specific constituent with a special problem, and tell how they helped that individual. This can both personalize them and demonstrate their desire to work hard for those who elected them.

Bill Quinn

I grew up in an editor's house. My dad Bill owned a business magazine company. But most of his early life he worked as a newspaper editor.

"What interests readers most is people," he emphasizes. "You can write about concepts and ideas, but readers relate best to other people, especially those who share their values, ideas, and problems.

"Names and details," he insists, "help the reader connect with the writer."

How to use these techniques in your daily work

Let's look at a number of daily writing chores, and put our new techniques to work solving them.

1. *School papers and essays.* The ideas of Socrates, Franklin, and Twain might all apply here. Sometimes, simply rephrasing an essay's question gives us a new perspective from which to write.

2. *Office memos and correspondence.* Politicians' styles might work well here. Lots of inter-office mail and e-mail requires single-theme focus, analogies that clarify the goals, a review of similar problems previously solved, and a reason some action should be taken.

3. *Sales letters.* My favorite letters follow Twain's secondary source approach or Socrates' question technique. Of course, in a sales letter, you want to ask questions for which you've got the answers.

4. *Speeches.* I favor Aristophanes' or Twain's approach here. However, in the places where

Aristophanes used rhymes, a modern speaker might use repeating phrases.

If you must choose between making a short or a long speech, I think shorter is better. And of course, sound bites today are critical. Can you add a memorable sound bite to your next talk?

Sermons can also be categorized as speeches. I once asked a minister friend, "What do you plan to talk about in next week's sermon?"

Knowing the beauty of brevity, he replied, "I am going to talk about 17 minutes."

5. *Newsletters*. If Ben Franklin were alive today, he'd likely be this country's premier newsletter publisher. Few authors have been able to combine his simple writing and ability to craft timeless sayings.

6. *Technical reports*. A wise educator once said that even a Ph.D. wants most material explained in basic language. Ben Franklin and Mark Twain both used simple words to teach complex lessons.

7. *Press releases and news stories*. Remember Bill Quinn's advice on names and details. Consider Will Rogers' use of topical material. Think about Aesop's ability to weave details into a memorable narrative.

The material that gets clipped from newspapers and magazines, then posted on bulletin boards, is generally a very short saying or story.

4
11 ways to write better (almost) instantly

I'm not particularly proud of this, but in school I always searched for "shortcuts." I looked for condensed books, easy-fix meals, and simple solutions to complex problems.

So, if you're looking for quick fixes for writing improvements, this is the chapter. But…don't stop there. You need to read the ALL of this book to get the most out of it…and for your readers to get the most out of you.

Following are a few simple solutions to solve complex writing dilemmas.

1. *Help readers see your thoughts* – The best writing tip I ever got: "Convert your thoughts into visual images." To

It took me 25 years to learn that there are two critical components of top-quality writing:

1. In the fast-paced 21st century, holding a reader's attention demands that you ENTERTAIN them. You can do this by telling a story that teaches a lesson, or one that offers a method to achieve a goal.

2. Virtually all writing is divided into four parts. In this book, we'll cover all of them in detail:

a. The title or heading.
b. The first sentence.
c. Transitional sentences and paragraphs – Those are the bridges that transport the reader from introduction to conclusion.
d. The ending or conclusion.

transport your ideas into someone else's mind, you must create verbal photos.

2. *The Quest* – Virtually all great stories – fiction or non-fiction -- describe a quest. The Three Little Pigs sought a well-built house. Peter Pan looked for his shadow. Dorothy searched for the Wizard of Oz.

3. *Unique experience* – Everyone has a different life story. Three popular approaches to tell that story include demonstrating (a) how someone overcame a problem, (b) a lesson an individual learned, or (c) a discovery the person made.

4. *Idea starters* – Great source for story ideas: look through TV schedules! For example, there are several "before and after" programs today that show how individuals redecorate homes or improve personal wardrobes. Could you use these formats to highlight an individual's story?

5. *Photo ideas* – When I'm asked to write company biographies, I request archival photos. I use those pictures to help owners and employees recall details from the company's early years.

6. *Biographical essay* – You may be asked to write essays for school projects. Later, you may need to produce multiple business reports. Almost any idea can be explained easier if it presents a human-interest story.

That story should contain at least three of the "Six P's." Here they are:

a. *Past* – This includes information about the subject's childhood, training, schooling, or early family life.

b. *Premonition* – Did the subject experience a feeling or early desire to go into a chosen occupation?

c. *Preparation* – This describes the subject's education and experiences, and how those prepared him/her for a specific profession.

d. *Pivotal event* – Was there a turning point or major event that changed the subject's life? How did the change come about?

e. *Present* – What is the subject doing today?

f. *Predictions* – Can the subject make certain professional assumptions or predictions based on his/her knowledge or experience?

7. *The title or headline* of a story is reportedly read up to five times more than body copy. That's why you absolutely *must* read Chapter 8.

8. *Those critical early paragraphs* – You gotta get the reader's attention! My favorite way is a combination of (a) Mark Twain's "episodic" formula and (b) the *declare and prepare* technique. (That's discussed in detail on page 70.)

    Twain's formula – Instead of moving chronologically from one event to another in his autobiography, Twain brilliantly talked about his life's most exciting episodes. To paraphrase this master storyteller, when he began to get bored with an episode, he simply moved on.

9. *Cliffhangers* – In many dramas, we see the main characters solve *one* problem, then face *another problem* which can't be solved until the next episode.

In movie serials of the 1940's and 1950's, this was called a cliffhanger. Why? The viewer might see the hero hanging from the edge of a cliff at the end of one episode. So…he had to return to the theater the next week to see how the hero escaped. (This book discusses that technique on page 45.)

10. *Write backwards* – If you've got the conclusion in mind, start building the story in a way that leads to that conclusion.

Here's one way to do it: *write your first paragraph LAST, after you've written the rest of the paper.* Since you know what you talked about in the rest of your essay, you can succinctly summarize it in that first paragraph. (You'll find much more about this on page 29.)

11. *The lesson* – When I interview someone, I take a cue from timeless stories. I often ask interviewees what lessons their biographies can teach others.

5
How *to use news, feature, and editorial writing styles*

If you write for your school paper or if you submit articles to publications, you're probably familiar with news, feature, and editorial writing styles.

In this chapter, we'll discuss these styles to show you some options when it comes to presenting your material, whether to a teacher, a boss, or a group.

The inverted pyramid (news style)

If you want to give your reader facts only, with no personal comments, this is a good approach.

It's called the "inverted pyramid" because the most important facts come right at the top of the story.

Imagine a pyramid turned upside down, resting on its point, with its large base at the top. That large base represents the major facts of the story: the who, what, when, where, why, and how. They're all presented in the first couple of paragraphs.

The remaining facts fall later. The idea here is to provide the reader all the major points she needs right at the first. Other details follow in descending order of importance.

A news style story about "The Three Bears" might begin something like this:

Papa Bear, 37, a homeowner living at 31 Tree Lane, reported a break-in to local authorities last night. When police arrived, they found a young woman, reportedly a minor, who identified herself as Goldilocks (no last name furnished).

The editorial style

As a student or employee, you are often asked to take a position on a subject or recommend an action of some sort.

That's why I prefer this style for what we address in the book: persuasive writing. We try to catch the reader's eye from the beginning. A viewpoint is usually taken, and evidence to support that view is presented.

In editorial style, other views may also be discussed, then refuted with evidence. In addition, a solution might be proposed, and the reader may be urged to take some action.

Let's revisit the "Bears" story applying this style:

A bizarre break-in at a private residence last night frightened a local bear family. But closer inspection by police indicates the illegal entry was triggered by little more than a juvenile's curiosity.

Does a trivial event like this really need to be reported? Let's look at some alleged break-ins recorded earlier this month.

Exercises to try

1. *Alter the pyramid.* Cut four or five pyramid-style stories from the newspaper. Rewrite each of

them emphasizing different facts from the original story. For instance, if the original story emphasizes an event (what), rewrite it emphasizing the person (who) or place (where).

2. *The feature that never happened.* Take a popular fairy tale or fable like "The Three Bears." Rewrite it as an editorial story, using the information we talked about earlier. For reference, you might use a current magazine or newspaper.

Another word on wordiness

Throughout this book you'll hear us scream, "cut, cut, cut." But don't cut during the first draft. That's when we want to get all our ideas for a particular news story or feature committed to paper.

Once we've got them down, then we can prioritize, cut, and refine our remarks.

6

6 ways to make your writing sizzle

Let's concentrate on several ways to build a story the reader can't put down. Then, we'll cap it with a great heading, and we've got a real eye-grabber.

Question: Where can you find examples of captivating, succinct writing?

The best place to hear powerful writing is on *radio*. Sure, music, talk, and interview shows abound. But next time you listen, pay special attention to the *advertisements*.

Here's the reason. To be effective, a radio message must make strong, instant impressions. It can reach only your sense of hearing. It cannot be reinforced by a vivid photo, an inviting smell, or by touch or taste.

Good radio writing engages you immediately. Even if you don't write for radio, we encourage you to pretend that you do. The best wordsmiths don't fear their words being spoken.

Accomplished writers in pre-radio times knew the power of sound. Says Abraham Lincoln scholar Charles Strozier, "Lincoln wrote to be read aloud."

1. Did you ever do this?

Back in school, if the teacher demanded a "term paper," I knew just what to do. I quickly researched the report, and wrote it as fast as I could.

Next, I reached for the thesaurus and looked up complicated, multisyllabic synonyms for my easy words. I made my paper cumbersome, obtuse, and so downright complex I couldn't understand it myself.

Wrong, wrong, wrong! But I didn't find that out until I wrote for a living. Then I discovered a most amazing thing. *If people don't understand something, they quit reading, watching, or listening.* There goes your audience.

Writing for the ear won't let you lose your reader. When you read something out loud, you hear not only the content, but the rhythm of the message. Anything that hinders comprehension and rhythm must be deleted.

Even if their lips don't move, many people still sound out each word they read silently. If it doesn't sound right aloud, think about changing it.

2. Listen up…to any station

The first step is to turn on the radio. It doesn't much matter which station. To stay on the air, most stations depend on advertising spots. So every few minutes you should hear several commercials. As you listen to each, ask yourself:

= Who is the advertiser? (And if you can't tell, that's bad!)

= What is the message or story about? Is it serious, funny, or seriously funny?

= How does the story turn out?

= Does the advertiser ask you to contact her?

= How does the advertiser suggest you make the contact? By phone or fax? By a visit to the Web site?

= If the advertiser doesn't give you contact information, what are you asked to do?

= Would you buy this product? Why or why not?

3. Next, become a radio commercial's ad writer

Take off your listener's hat, and put on your writer's hat. Keep these things in mind as you create the commercial:

The first few words are critical. They must capture the listener's attention immediately. Some commercials do it by asking a question. Others make a profound or surprising statement. (Example: "I slept better last night than I ever have before. Want to know why?")

Most ads make an offer or a promise right up front. (Example: "In the next two minutes you'll hear three secrets to help you make more money, day in, day out.")

The most effective ads make one single point. Everything else in the ad reinforces that one thing. (Example: "If you need insurance right now, listen closely. The next minute could save you thousands.")

Sometimes commercials use two voices. One might be the announcer or questioner. The other might offer a "testimonial," discussing how the product or service worked for a customer.

Strong ad copy often creates a buying mood by instilling a hunger for the product. This might be developed rationally (giving logical reasons to buy) or emotionally (telling how the product might enhance sex appeal, social status, etc.).

An engaging radio spot usually urges the listener to take immediate action. Perhaps it asks him to visit a restaurant, and describes its location near a local landmark. Or, it briefly discusses five reasons to buy a car now, then gives a toll-free number you can call for details.

Major points of the radio spot are often repeated, especially the action step that asks the listener to act. If the action step is calling a toll-free phone number, that number might be repeated two or three times.

4. Wrapping the audio package

Some radio spots last only 30 seconds. Many are one minute, some last two. The average speaking rate is about 120 words a minute, give or take 20 words.

So, a 30-second spot would contain about 60 words, a one-minute spot 120 words, and a two-minute ad 240 words.

Almost any single-themed message can be delivered in 250 words or less. That includes radio or TV spots, and short news stories you send to magazines or newspapers. Abe Lincoln could do it…why can't you?

5. A sample commercial

Let's package everything now in a two-minute ad. In this example, we'll present a mythical company, RQ Writing Service.

=========================

Are you a qualified, experienced professional who's been laid off due to budget cuts?

That's what happened to me five years ago. And that's the reason I started RQ Writing Service—to help qualified people like you find good jobs quickly.

We offer more than just a piece of paper with your work experience. First, we interview you to uncover the one or two special qualities that make you a valuable prospect.

Next, we help you find industries where your special skills fit best. Then we help you prepare a single-page resume that speaks to those industries.

Now, let me share a secret with you. There are still plenty of good jobs out there if you know where to look.

That's why we maintain close relationships with three major job placement companies. Not only can we write your resume, we can put your resume in the right hands, too!

Word Smith, a copywriter we placed in a lucrative technical writing job, says, "RQ Writing

Service turned my life around for less money than I'd spend on a weekend trip."

Give us a chance. And if you're dissatisfied, the resume is free!

Call us today toll-free at 000-000-0000. That's 000-000-0000. When you do, we'll send you a free report on repackaging your skills for the 21st century.

RQ Writing Service. We help qualified people find quality jobs.

= =

6. Keep things simple and concrete

Note that in this message the words and concepts are exceedingly concrete and basic. There's nothing abstract, ethereal, or visionary here. This is simple writing.

The key is understandability. *If the reader or listener can't understand, he'll quit reading or listening.*

7
14 techniques for creating a two-minute masterpiece

1. Conclusion first – the "writing backwards" technique

Some say this technique—where the writer determines a conclusion first, then builds the rest of the story to support it—began with ancient dramatists creating stories for the stage.

In the late 1800's, it's reported that author Horatio Alger, Jr. popularized this technique with novels of young men overcoming adversity through honesty, hard work, and determination.

You can use this method to create school themes, book reports, press releases, corporate biographies, and much more.

Let's say you want to develop a story about that resume service we just discussed. Where do you start?

a. Take a single sheet of paper, and write down all the advantages the service offers potential customers. (Personal interview with job applicant, a huge database of job openings, etc.)

b. Next, rank those attributes, or benefits, from most important to least important.

c. Now, here's the hard part. Pick the best attribute. This can become your first sentence or a powerful enticement for your heading.

Let's say, in the case of my mythical resume writing service, the major benefit I offer is "helping qualified people find jobs quickly." Virtually everything I discuss in the radio ad reinforces my background of providing support for job applicants.

d. Now, write your report. Each benefit is explained in a single paragraph, and since you've prioritized them, the document is developed in descending order.

Or, you may choose to focus on only one or two attributes. Generally, I like to emphasize rare or unusual attributes that other services may not offer.

e. End the story with a paragraph that reinforces the major point in the heading and first paragraph.

f. Finally, to check your work, ask co-workers or friends to read it, and see if their summations agree with yours.

2. Some popular storytelling methods

= Effective stories often begin with a problem that needs to be solved, and subsequent paragraphs discuss benefits from the solution.

= Stories can use a syllogism. That is, they give a major premise, and a minor premise that develops from the major one. Finally, the stories summarize the findings with a conclusion.

For example, most resume services offer a good employment database. But ours focuses mainly on local jobs:

We want to help you find a better career without having to leave family, friends, and this great community.

= Sometimes a case study method works. A satisfied-customer story, for instance, might detail one person's problem, and tell how your product solved it. (Of course, to use that person's name and quote, it's important to get his or her written permission first.)

= Most people enjoy success stories, about how others either avoid loss or win. Can you incorporate one of these ideas into your report?

= Here's a critical secret, perhaps one of the most important we'll cover. A key to capturing readers is *discussing common troubles*.

You'll note that many comedians begin routines by bringing up a gripe or grievance. Can you talk about a problem we all might confront, then tell how your product or service solved it?

Clichés—those common expressions everyone knows—are frequently criticized. But vivid, familiar phrases often help readers remember concepts better.

Can you fill in the following clichés? (1) Fit as a _____. (2) Busy as a _____. (3) Read between the _____. (4) Turn over a new _____. (5) A bird in the _____.

3. Repetition

Now, just for a moment, imagine yourself on an elevator. Huh?

Yep, you step aboard and you hear some old song, then the door opens and you walk out singing it.

Why is this? Hypnosis? How did you remember this old, old song? Maybe because (1) it's simple, (2) the chorus repeats, and (3) it either surprises you or tells a memorable story.

Now, think back to some of humankind's "greatest hits." You know, the timeless messages generations repeat to one another. Want examples?

Martin Luther King, Jr.'s speech at the Lincoln Memorial is named for the phrase he used repeatedly, "I have a dream."

Edgar Allan Poe's enthralling poem "The Raven" ends several stanzas with the line "Quoth the raven, 'Nevermore.'"

Listen to radio commercials again. Note repetition of things like phone numbers and Web sites.

4. Use active verbs

An active verb does just what the name implies: it takes action. Its counterpart, the passive verb, simply exists. Passive verb examples: is, was, were.

The best writing never simply exists. It flows, runs, climbs, jumps, flies. Or, to create mood, it might meander, stroll, or dance.

Some experts suggest working as many senses (sound, taste, sight, smell, touch) into a story as possible, so the reader can visualize what's happening.

5. Create audience involvement—The Winky Dink Story

Each afternoon, we hunkered down next to the TV and waited for a cartoon boy who needed our help.

In the 1950s and 1960s, Winky Dink wowed kids by getting into more jams than a taste-tester at a jelly convention. Winky and his dog Woofer moved from one adventure to another.

Basic cartoon fare, right? Wrong! Because when Winky found trouble, viewers like me bailed him out. How?

Have you ever seen the magic screen? Winky fans ordered one through the mail. This little plastic sheet attached to your TV screen, sort of like sandwich wrap. Now comes the secret.

Let's say Winky falls into the ocean, OK? So he's drowning, and this voice says, "Winky needs a boat." Dots appear on the TV screen. Real quick, viewers connect the dots with a crayon, drawing a boat. Winky climbs in, and he's saved. Wow!

Now, what if you at home don't connect those dots? Does Winky drown? Nah, but if you're six years old, you may not know that.

And so it goes, throughout the show. Winky digs himself a hole, and you draw the ladder that pulls him out, or the shovel that helps him find the gold, and so on.

Then sometime in the cartoon, there's a secret message. First, dots for the tops of letters appear, and you connect them. Then these dots leave the screen, and new dots forming the bottoms of letters show up, and you connect these.

Now you've got a full message. Maybe it's just "Eat your vegetables," but hey, it's secret!

What magic formula did Winky unearth?

Edwin Brit Wyckoff and Harry W. Prichett created Winky nearly 50 years ago. Today, we recognize this as perhaps TV's first interactive program.

This interaction compels us to do more than sit back, listen, and watch. We get involved. We relate to the action, and influence its outcome.

Can interactivity create reader loyalty? I think so. But along with interaction, you must offer the reader:

a. A reason to connect with you. If you talk about an idea, or a candidate, how can the reader get more information on that subject? A toll-free number? A Web site?

b. A memorable connective tool. If you edit a school newspaper, you can encourage reader letters. If you write a column for that paper, you could turn it into an advice column, prompting readers to ask questions to which you respond. Or, could you start a club for others who share your interest?

6. Analogy or comparison

The analogy is a way to point out similarities. What if a time machine deposited you back in the Middle Ages, and you had to explain baseball to a knight?

"To play baseball," you might begin, "you'll need a bat."

"What, knave?" he'd query. "You mean a flying bat, like a vampire bat?"

"No," you'd counter, "this bat is a long wooden stick. You would use it to hit a sphere."

"You are crazy!" he'd argue. "Everyone knows a stick offers little protection from a spear."

Oops! Now you're forced come up with an analogy (a similarity) for baseball. One comparative technique is the simile, an explicit comparison using the words "like" or "as." Example: "Baseball is a sports contest, like fencing or archery."

Another way to do this would be through a metaphor, an implicit comparison that speaks of one thing as if it were another. Example: "Baseball is a test of throwing and hitting skills."

7. Anecdotes and testimonials

My friend raved about his boss all the time. "She knows I'm still in school," he said, "so she always asks about my schedule.

"Not only that," he ranted, "she's really smart, too. The company wants to promote her, but she keeps telling them she really trained to teach. She's just waiting for a job opening."

"Hey," I stopped him, "if she's so great, why don't you take her out?"

"Nah," he said. "She's too old for me."

"So, how old is she?" I shot back. "30...40...more?"

"Nope, she's 23. That's about right for you. Want me to get you a date with her?"

Not wanting to appear desperate -- which I was -- I hesitated, then said, "I guess that's OK. How about tomorrow?"

Well, he set us up.

Did the date work out? Absolutely. Nearly three decades later we're still happily married.

Frankly, I'm amazed, bothered, and bewildered that advertisers don't use testimonials or appropriate anecdotes more often to add credibility to the writing.

Not long ago, a friend spoke to a college class. He's a small business owner, so the students peppered him with questions about inventories, salaries, hiring, and then about marketing.

"One thing I do," he said, "is to ask satisfied customers to write me testimonials.

"In fact," he continued, "maybe you should ask for recommendations from former employers, and send them out when you graduate and start your job hunt."

The students acted surprised. They laughed at him.

"Are you kidding?" said one. "I'd be embarrassed to do that. I mean, my resume tells everything I've done."

"Well," my friend replied, "a resume is your opinion of yourself. A testimonial, however, is someone else's validation. Which one do you think will carry more weight?"

8. Turning points

A few years ago, I talked to a bicycle dealer who invented a machine that straightens bent bike wheels. "Wow," I marveled, "what gave you this incredible idea?"

"Strange as it seems," he explained, "the idea hit me at the city dump. I was throwing a bunch of wheels away, and recalled a conversation I had with my dad.

"Whenever he'd discard a wheel, he'd say, 'There must be a better solution than this.'"

That dealer returned to his shop and created a great new item, one that saved other retailers both wheels and money.

What's the "turning point" of your story? Could you use it to help others, or to teach a lesson? Could you use it to begin your story?

9. Point out the flaws first

My mother's father died before I was born. One day I asked my dad about him.

"Before he passed away," Dad remembered, "he'd built a good real estate clientele. He sold lots of houses, in a very unique way."

"How's that?" I asked.

"Old Tom had an eye for detail. When a house came on the market, he got there early and went over it with a fine-tooth comb. No imperfection escaped his eye, and he wrote down whatever he saw.

"When a prospective buyer asked his opinion on a property, Tom pulled out his flaw sheet. At a glance, the prospect could see everything that was wrong."

Strangely, prospects might begin to defend this problem property! Wait a minute, they might think. For only a few thousand bucks, this house could be a showplace.

Tom's honesty and eye for errors won him new customers, and led to fewer complaints after the sale.

What's wrong with this picture? Often, we get so emotionally invested in our idea, we disregard the down side. Yet, that's what scares most readers—or prospective buyers—off.

How can we present our reader a flaw sheet? Some writers do it right up front, in the early paragraphs:

= =

Jerry Sharpshooter claims his camera store sits on the worst retail location in the county. "It's off the main road, three miles out of town, and hard to find if you don't look for it," Jerry laughs.

So, to repay a customer for the driving inconvenience, Jerry offers some of the best prices in the state on...

==

Begin your "flaw list" with these questions:

a. What's the biggest complaint/argument against your idea?

Every time you sit down to write, remember...
1. The reader is a very busy person.

2. That reader is likely to be doing something else, like watching TV or talking to someone, while he's studying your material.

3. The reader gets exposed to hundreds of messages a day. Unless you tell her something wonderful, exciting, surprising, or funny, you may not keep her attention.

4. A high percentage of readers look at your heading and first sentence only, so those may be your only opportunities to establish a connection.

*5. MOST IMPORTANT— Many folks tell me
writing is like staging a play. The writer must
instantly catch the reader's attention, surprise or
amuse him constantly with clever words or change
of pace, then provide him with a logical
conclusion.*

b. What's the most disastrous thing that could
happen if your idea is carried out?

c. Is your idea or service expensive? What would
make people initially reject it?

d. If you gave a speech about your idea, what
questions would people ask?

e. What has your competition said about your
idea?

   Armed with this knowledge, you can create a
powerful argument that will address the
weaknesses first, then tell how you've solved
them.
   Prioritize the complaints by using the "writing
backwards" method we discussed earlier. That
Number 1 complaint can become the focus of your
countering argument.

10. Vaudeville…warm-ups and surprises
   Long before the Internet, cell phones, and TV,
vaudeville entertainment captivated this nation.
From the 1870s until the movie talkies and radio
took over in the 1930s, performers toured the

country telling jokes, dancing, or juggling
anything they could lift.

More details about vaudeville…

*The earliest American variety shows originated
in saloons, where owners hired entertainers to
bring patrons in and keep 'em longer. But as
shows became more elaborate, they moved into
theaters.*

*Vaudeville offered something for all ages, and
became family entertainment. Booking agents,
representing a number of performers, put together
shows with appealing mixtures of music,
acrobatics, comedy, dancing, and occasionally a
lecture!*

*The performers traveled a circuit around the
country, so theaters got a brand new show every
week or two.*

*The bill might include 8 to 15 or even 20 acts.
The next-to-last performer was the "headliner."
That was a tough act to follow, because when the
headliner left, much of the crowd did, too.*

*Sadly, this wonderful entertainment form died
when budgets tightened during the Depression,
radio moved into living rooms, and theaters opted
for movies over live performers.*
Source: www.lazervaudeville.com

What tricks did performers employ to keep the
folks amused?

a. *The warm-up*. A master of ceremonies or warm-up act got the crowd excited, or prepared them for the festivities about to happen. "Hold on to your seats," he'd say. "You're about to see the most amazing act in stage history."

b. *Constant surprise*. Jugglers, acrobats, magicians, and ventriloquists wowed the crowd, and comedians offered outrageous (but clean) gags.

c. *Audience involvement*. Often, the performer would bring a local person up on stage, simultaneously creating audience interaction and connecting with townspeople.

Try these vaudeville techniques to hold readers:

a. Tell readers you're about to say something important, and why they'll benefit by listening to it.

b. Surprise the reader by offering either new information or information packaged in a new way.

c. Involve the readers by giving details on how to get more information, or why they should maintain contact with you.

11. Provocative or outrageous statements

Next to infomercial actors, talk show hosts are the fastest-growing population on earth. Why?

On both radio and TV, talk shows are relatively inexpensive to produce. Except for a few national programs, few require elaborate sets or scripts, and many guests are eager to appear. Fans -- often listening in the car -- like the free-flowing patter and unpredictable phone calls.

I have the greatest respect for these folks, especially radio hosts. Not because I share their beliefs, but because it's extremely tough to fill three hours with interesting conversation.

How do hosts keep an audience tuned in?

a. They take a position on an issue. They present a definite opinion, then ask callers to respond to it.

b. They book provocative guests. I heard one guy claim to be a space alien who insisted that many from his planet lived on earth, disguised as car hood ornaments.

c. They promote upcoming segments. When close to break or commercial time, hosts often remind listeners, "We'll find out about Joe's secret life…right after this message."

d. They offer answers. Did you notice how many show hosts are problem solvers? They propose a common problem, invite listeners to call in, then offer solutions.

e. They offer a reason to tune in to their next show.

Talk show hosts know you can't excite an audience by whispering. Take a position, offer an answer to a problem, keep your audience (readers) involved.

12. Quotations

To quote Hendrik Willem Van Loon, "Somewhere in the world there is an epigram for every dilemma." Or, to quote Socrates, "A short saying often contains much wisdom."

You can use a quote to add more impact to your argument. (And you can quote me on that.)

Two of my favorite books of quotes are *The Penguin Dictionary of Modern Humorous Quotations* compiled by Fred Metcalf, and *The International Thesaurus of Quotations* compiled by Rhoda Thomas Tripp.

13. Humor

I've put this near the bottom of the list, because it's really tricky.

Ever see a stand-up comic test jokes? I've witnessed several, and it's a brutal process.

The comic begins by facing a crowd with several jokes written on index cards or note paper. If the card gets a laugh, the comic saves it. If not, he junks it.

Trouble is, humor is extremely personal. What's funny to you isn't always funny to me, and vice versa.

If you want to try it, here are some basic joke forms:

a. *Play-on-words*. Among the corniest. Let me be frank with you. Although Frank is not my name.

b. *Non-sequitur*. Some insects have two wings, others have four. Wingless insects like ants don't fly. They carpool.

c. *Exaggeration*. No one knows how many insects exist because some fly into bug zappers, some live underground, and some fall beneath shoes. But, the last approximate count was 387 gazillion.

d. *Comparative*. It was so cold today that...

e. Set up and punch line. I asked the cook, "Can you make a catfish?" And the cook said, "Well, I could give him a rod and reel, but I'm not sure he can use it."

My favorite books on humor are *Comedy Writing Secrets* by Melvin Helitzer and *Comedy Writing Step-by-Step* by Gene Perret.

14. Cliffhangers

About fifty years ago, movie serials—also called continuing stories—kept theater crowds returning week after week. Each episode ended with a cliffhanger, a suspenseful, unresolved problem. You'd need to come back the following week to find out what happened.

But history reminds us that this form flourished during the Middle Ages. Storytellers journeyed from castle to castle, spinning suspenseful yarns without end. (What a way to guarantee return appearances!)

Daytime television offers much the same thing with soap operas.

Writers often create cliffhangers by (1) defining a potential problem, (2) telling how to solve it, (3) stating the solution might lead to another problem, (4) solving that one, but pointing to another problem, and so on.

For example, the three little pigs grow up, crowding the house. (Problem) Their mom suggests they move out. (Solution)

But now the pigs must build their own homes. (Problem) The first little pig builds a straw house. (Solution) But the wolf blows it down. (Problem)…etc., etc.

See how this works? Isn't it cool? See how situation comedies use this? See how you could use this?

8
51 ways to create an awesome title or heading

Suppose you pick up the paper tomorrow and see this headline: "Police begin campaign to run down jaywalkers."

Heck, I'll scan this story just to see if they've run over any of my friends! But wait, maybe the article means something else. Ah, yes, perhaps the police just want to ticket these folks!

But guess what? I'm already into the story. Like a giant vacuum, that weird headline sucked me right into the first paragraph. Because, like a vacuum, I'm looking for dirt! OK, maybe not dirt. But for gossip, or strange news, or stuff nobody else knows.

Following are some more wild headlines. (I believe they're real. Many were sent to me by e-mail.) If you saw these unusual nuggets, would you read the story that followed?

Panda mating fails; veterinarian takes over

Teacher strikes idle kids

Juvenile court to try shooting defendant

Dealers will hear car talk at noon

If strike isn't settled quickly, it may last awhile

Cold wave linked to temperatures

Two sisters reunite after 18 years at checkout counter

Red tape holds up new bridges

Typhoon rips through cemetery; hundreds dead

Squad helps dog bite victim

New study of obesity looks for larger test group

Headline sources: various papers, www.slinkycity.com

Research tells us that people read headlines about four times more often than they read body copy. Yet many writers—myself included—spend much more time agonizing over the story than the title. Duh! What's wrong with us?

Did you notice something else about these titles? All of them are slightly incongruous. They just don't quite make sense. That's what forces us to read more.

Words for the wise

It's reported that a major university conducted a study to find the English language's 12 most persuasive words. They were:
(1) you, (2) money, (3) save, (4) new, (5) results, (6) easy, (7) health, (8) safety, (9) love, (10) discovery, (11) proven, and (12) guarantee.

I've always been told that the strongest word in a headline is the verb. And many claim the more active the verb, the better! Would these action words enhance school paper and theme headings, too? Probably.

Which heading would make you read more? "John Player wins game with touchdown" or "John Player's diving catch clinches playoffs."

Road signs, stop signs, and headlines

Picture yourself cruising down the highway. Left and right, huge signboards appear, then vanish as you drive past them. Occasionally, one or two catch your eye. Do you remember any of them?

Experts tell us these signs should be ten words or less. Otherwise, they could be both confusing and a traffic hazard.

Ask people who drove cars in the 1940s, '50s, and '60s which road signs they recall best. Most likely they'll say Burma Shave.

This shaving cream company created a series of messages that dotted the highways all over America. Each complete message required five or six small signs to reveal part of the story.

Each sign held only four or five words. The last sign revealed the sponsor: Burma Shave.

When writing your headline, think about Burma Shave's method. Catch the reader's attention, but reveal only part of the message. Save the rest of the details for the story.

Another way to look at titles: the "Stop" sign perspective. We see hundreds of signs every day, but when we see the familiar red, six-sided stop sign, we do what we're told.

Your headline should do this too—force the reader to stop and look before going further.

Headings as advertisements

One more way to sell your heading: Consider your story's theme as a product. Certainly politicians do this, appealing to as many voters' needs as they can. In fact, these office-seekers often present themselves the same way as a box of cereal or a new set of tires—good for everyone, or safe on bumpy roads.

Which of these basic human needs does your idea or service benefit?

a. Comfort and convenience, b. Sexual attractiveness, c. Security of family or dwelling, d. Freedom from fear, e. Health and long life, f. Social acceptance, g. Exclusivity, h. Recreation or play, i. Cleanliness, orderliness, j. Speed or efficiency, k. Dependability or quality, l. Style or beauty, m. Curiosity (one of my favorites).

51 ways to showcase your story with a heading:

1. *Begin with the words who, what, when, where, why, or how.* Who really won in "Three Little Pigs" story? or How to keep your home safe from windy wolves.

2. *Offer a test.* Do you have these problems? or Do you have symptoms of _____?

3. *Make a rhyme*. Three pigs frolic and play after wolf runs away.

4. *The long list*. Ten ways to improve your golf or Thirteen ways to find out if…

5. *How to*. How to captivate readers with your first few words.

6. *Real reason*. The real reason two houses blew down.

7. *Don't do this*. If you want a safer house, don't do this.

8. *Big problem*. How Pig # 3 solved his chimney problem.

9. *Straight talk*. The straight scoop on tasty ice cream.

10. *Accidental discovery*. Accidental discovery of ancient pottery leads scientists to historic site.

11. *What if*. What if your house blew down tomorrow?

12. *New help*. New help for dry skin.

13. *Savings*. Part-time student saves two hours a day.

14. *Rapid learning*. Pig learns to build safe house in 12 days.

15. *Startling fact.* Pig reveals startling facts about wolf's lung capacity.

16. *Opposites.* Pig learns good lesson from bad experience.

17. *At last.* After 100 years, new study of "Three Pigs" reveals author at last.

18. *Percentage or fraction.* Two out of three readers believe fairy tales are true.

19. *Shock or outrage.* Townspeople shocked by "Three Pigs" story.

20. *Fault or blame.* Judge says wolf attack not pigs' fault.

21. *Strange or odd.* Strange sounds leave citizens worried.

22. *Quick fix.* Two-minute test offers amazing results.

23. *Categories or types.* Researcher asks: Which type are you?

24. Prognostication. Broker predicts improved stock market by next week.

25. *Inside secrets or tips.* Escape secrets revealed by pigs.

26. *Open letter*. Pigs send open letter to wolf community.

27. *Pass this test*. Could you pass this fitness challenge?

28. *What's wrong*. What's wrong with this story?

29. *Simplicity*. Body builder tells simple way to keep fit.

30. *Ought to know or must know*. What you must know about chimneys.

31. *Specific day, date, or time*. July 4 means parades, celebrations in our town.

32. *Problem question*. Fallen arches? Here's one overlooked reason.

33. *Imagine*. What will life be like in 2050?

34. *Nostalgia*. Local citizen remembers days before cars.

35. *Breakthrough*. Social worker announces breakthrough research on homelessness.

36. *Start from scratch*. How local mosquito repellent company started from scratch.

37. *Mistake*. The mistake that cost one teen a scholarship.

38. *Time pressure*. Quick study methods revealed for students short on time.

39. *Right and wrong*. Right and wrong ways to drive discussed.

40. *The unexpected*. New aging research contradicts last year's results.

41. *Before and after*. Pigs view wolves differently after break-ins.

42. *News from experts*. Advice to nervous people from relaxation expert.

43. *Wild, crazy luck*. Local waiter finds 1997 lottery ticket worth thousands.

44. *Long struggle, late success*. After 30-year struggle, man denied schooling now reads well.

45. *Building momentum*. Playoff foes share history of hard-fought competitions.

46. *Privileged lifestyle*. Jet-set weekends common for movie star.

47. *The dating game*. Dating etiquette for the 21st century.

48. *Battle of the sexes*. Number 1 reason men won't ask for directions.

49. *Setting a standard.* Local umpire sets high standards for fair play and sportsmanship.

50. *Crazy mix-up.* Error on application form creates hopeless confusion for woman during interview.

51. *The moral.* Pennies really do make dollars says local coin collector.

As you scan this list, think about all the ways these headers could be altered slightly to fit your idea or product. And remember that the best headings may often ask a question that can be answered by the story, prompt the reader to beg, "Tell me more," appeal to the reader's current needs, and, most importantly, offer new information.

Four postscripts on the headline
1. Pretend you have to highlight the story to your reader, but you can use only ten words. Then, select those words that name the subject, briefly describe the action taken, and hint at the focus of the paper. For example, Magician Joe Rabbit reveals five secrets of holding a crowd.

2. For student themes and reports, you might experiment with heading number 8 (big problem), 15 (startling fact), 35 (breakthrough), 40 (the unexpected), and 51 (the moral). A heading for a report about Tom Sawyer's fence-painting episode

might be How Tom Sawyer showed friends that work can be fun.

3. We're often asked what headline messages work best for office memos, business reports, and e-mail transmissions.

For office memos, you might try headers like Have you seen this? or Are you interested in this? For some reason (unknown to me), people often respond to a headline question by quickly scanning the following paragraphs for the answer.

Regarding e-mails, in my own correspondence I use only three or four words that fit on a single line. I keep total letter count (including letters and the spaces in between) under 30 characters.

Reason? I want my entire headline to appear in the subject portion of the recipient's inbox. (Some people like to keep e-mail headers under 25 characters!)

4. Headings that relate to a specific person often draw a reader into the story. Abe Lincoln's early tragedies is likely to draw more attention than How one president coped with problems.

9
How to captivate your reader in the first sentence

Here, we'll focus on the early part of your feature story: the first sentence or two. Along with the heading or headline, it's the most important part.

Copywriting experts insist the headline's main purpose is to make the reader read the first sentence. The first sentence should be so good it sticks to the reader's mind like duct tape.

Why getting those first words just right matters

Pretend for a moment you're a talent scout sitting in a small room. At 9 a.m. the door opens, and 100 entertainers race in. All begin their acts simultaneously.

Some sing, a few dance, one juggles, another walks on her hands, still another one swings from the overhead light. What a madhouse.

Your readers face similar distractions. Of all the reports or stories available to them, how do they decide which ones to read?

What is really critical?

In some corporations, managers are given information on a need-to-know basis. They're provided data only if it relates directly to their areas of responsibility.

We writers should follow this rule. But often we don't. In sharing new information with a reader, we often provide too much history and background the reader doesn't need to know. All this superfluous junk bores the reader before she can get excited about our real story.

If you focus too much on the background, the main subject of your story slips OUT of focus.

60 ways to make the reader stay with you
To see how other writers start a story, surround yourself with newspapers and magazines. Don't look for straight news (the who, what, where, when, why, and how stories).

Instead, you want to emulate features or editorials. Gather 15 or 20 features with particularly well-written first sentences.

What do they have in common? When I tried this, here's what I found.

1. *Repeat the headline using different words.* If the original headline says Local citizen welcomes space aliens your first sentence might proclaim The local sheriff says space visitors are welcome at his home.

2. *Suggest an alternative.* For folks who don't have the time or inclination to devote two hours daily to studying the stock market, here's a possible alternative.

3. *Set a scene.* Researchers gathered in a packed laboratory today to hear results of the latest study on the common cold.

4. *Present new evidence*. Experts have spent years telling us exercise helps. But new evidence suggests you can get too much of a good thing.

5. *Offer new hope*. For aging baby boomers, there's new hope for a vaccine that slows aging in lab rats.

6. *Ask why*. Why do you always remember where you left the keys, but never remember where you left the car?

7. *Reveal a discovery*. While biking through the woods last month, I made a discovery that changed my life.

8. *Recall a certain day*. "Yesterday, December 7, 1941, a date that will live in infamy, the naval and air forces..." -- Franklin D. Roosevelt

9. *Relate an unforgettable event*. I'll never forget the day I met my wife. Alternatively, often used in speeches: I'll always remember...

10. *Predict or tell of a premonition*. Little did I know when I entered that room what I was about to discover.

11. *Use fear or horror*. "The dog's missing," Dad said, and I froze in my tracks.

12. *Reveal the magic keys*. A high school baseball coach has developed five keys to a perfect swing.

13. *Examine a ritual.* For 50 years, former grads have returned to the old abandoned high school building at Homecoming to share memories of their school days.

14. *Offer a checklist.* Don't leave the office before trying these five techniques designed to help you work more efficiently.

15. *Share a shortcut.* Here's a method to race through a book, absorb the main points, and cut your reading time by half.

16. *Emphasize ease.* Here are three easy ways to check your carpet for mildew.

17. *Explain cause and effect.* If you've got a foot problem, it could be coming from one of these stress-related activities.

18. *Describe a problem and its solution.* Bob used to have trouble understanding conversations in a crowded room. Now, he's found a method to hear better.

19. *Induce action by a time constraint.* If you have these symptoms of lung disease, contact your doctor soon.

20. *Disprove an old saying.* Whoever said "You can't see the forest for the trees" must have looked in the wrong direction.

21. *Give free advice.* Free advice for the new father is as near as a computer Web site.

22. *Differ from the norm.* Looking at the tall, slim Texan, you'd never guess he played defensive tackle in high school.

23. *Contrast.* John expected to feel much worse following the knee replacement, but thanks to modern techniques and these exercises, he improved quickly.

24. *What would you do?* Suppose you found yourself stuck on a dark country road late at night with no cell phone? What would you do?

25. *Gaze upon the private person.* Senator Smith moves confidently through the crowd, smiling and shaking hands. Few know the shy youth inside, who struggled against many obstacles to reach his present position.

26. *Stress the unbelievable.* Outsiders can't believe the conditions in this city's schools. Experts say these crumbling structures need immediate attention.

27. *Make immediate with the present tense.* Larry smiles to himself as he jogs up the mountain. Every day he finds new scenery here.

28. *Number the content.* Next time you're hungry, try one of these ten proven one-minute recipes.

29. *How I started.* My first acting job paid nothing. It was a second grade school play.

30. *Where are they now?* David Sportsman rarely comes to the ballpark anymore, because his new job gives him even more satisfaction than hitting home runs.

31. *Consider the average.* The average person travels 3.4 miles on foot during the day, but…

32. *Display history repeating itself.* The student walk-out yesterday seemed a radical move to new teachers, but not to veteran educators who recalled October of 1969.

33. *Something's not right.* Last week, when Joe searched his car for the contracts, he worried when he found them under his briefcase, not in the passenger seat where he left them.

34. *Trivia.* Here's information on the new football stadium for trivia buffs.

35. *Surprises.* If you always considered this town boring, wait until you hear about the surprises found in the 1933 time capsule unearthed at city hall last week.

36. *Which did you choose?* (This could also be called "Take this test.") What type are you? Answer the following 15 questions to find out if you're an introvert or an extrovert.

37. *Word from the expert.* Weather watcher Bob Maelstrom has correctly predicted the temperature on Thanksgiving for 30 years. What does he prognosticate this November?

38. *Convincing evidence.* Recent voter pattern studies offer convincing evidence that the incumbent mayor will win reelection.

39. *Great idea.* Susan Bee, a junior at the high school, revealed a new homecoming plan both students and teachers applaud.

40. *Don't let this happen.* Failure to check for a spare tire left one councilman miles away from a critical meeting last week.

41. *Good news or alleviation of worry.* Citizens who worried that the zoo might be closed can now breathe easier. An anonymous citizen has agreed to donate funds to pay for the needed repairs.

42. *Best lesson learned.* The college's football coach claims the most valuable lesson he learned came not on the field, but in an English class.

43. *Working together.* Last year this town endured a devastating flood. What steps can we take to prevent it this year?

44. *Defying the odds.* Suffering a bruised calf in early September, quarterback Tom Touchdown saw little hope he'd be leading his team in October.

45. *Road to success.* This year's valedictorian says he followed a five-step daily study method, which he shared with reporters who covered the graduation ceremony.

46. *Dream comes true.* How many of us aspire to be a state champion of anything? When Lisa Jogger began training for cross-country running, she never imagined how far she'd travel.

47. *Now hear this.* A national committee on aging unanimously agreed that the following 15 suggestions might actually make everyone healthier.

48. *Guessing game.* Can you guess the three things people worry about most often?

49. *The legend.* Legendary radio announcer Mark Microphone addressed 10,000 fans at the convention center last night, and offered tips for anyone wanting to present a message more clearly and effectively.

50. *Shared traits.* What traits do we share with insects, and how have they helped us survive?

51. *Shifting gears/radical departure.* Movie idol David Film shifts personalities completely for his next starring role.

52. *The new category.* Pop singer Tiffany Audio exemplifies a whole group of young performers who share several unique traits.

53. *Is she alive?* Former 1940s starlet Jean Screen appeared in town last week for the first time in 60 years. Or did she?

54. *Unexpected occurrence.* Who'd expect an 83-year-old, who started exercising only five years ago, to take first place in 2002's citywide one-mile walk?

55. *Uncanny ability.* High school scholar Mark Algebra claims his consistently high classroom scores are based on his skill at recalling -- almost word-for-word -- lectures by his teachers.

56. *What do you really know?* Most townspeople know Main Street can pose major traffic hazards, but what do we really know statistically about accident frequency there?

57. *Like mother, like daughter.* Twenty-five years ago, Sheila Smart took first place in the town spelling bee. This year, her daughter Lisa returned the title to the family.

58. *Ever think about this?* Do you ever think about life on other planets? Many experts say it exists, but it's much different from ours.

59. *Strange but true*. A new research technique claims 79% effectiveness in predicting future events.

60. *Reunions*. After 40 years living separate lives, twin brothers reunited here last week, and found they had much in common.

The secret of first paragraphs

The power of the first sentence or two is simply this: It makes every reader ask "What happens next?" or say "Really? Tell me more."

It briefly explains what the rest of the article is all about. If the first paragraph does not convincingly lead to the next paragraph, it should be rewritten.

Now you've got 60 ways to begin your story.

There's an old journalism yarn about a young reporter who's assigned his first editorial. Knowing this should be an opinion article, he takes a strong stand, lacing his article with expressions like "I think," "I'm convinced that," and "In this writer's opinion."

The editor, who's trained hundreds of aspirants, tells him, "Bob, I really like this piece. It's well researched, persuasive, nicely written.

"But you know what would make it better? Let your subject do more talking. Add more third-person quotes, other opinions that complement yours."

If you want readers to agree with you, don't lecture them, show them. In short, avoid the "I" on your keyboard.

10
How to build your case, and then close it

In Chapter 9, we covered 60 ways to begin your short feature. Each of those first sentences should make the reader ask, "What happens next?" Good question. How do you supply the answer?

When we create words that stick, we're also building paragraphs that stick. That means every sentence should build on the previous one.

Memorable prose builds step by step, magically pulling the reader from the heading into the first paragraph, then through the story to the conclusion.

The condensation consideration

Many of us think in terms of volume. We figure the more evidence we pile on, the stronger the case. *But history's most powerful word artists remind us that in most instances, brevity triumphs.*

Probably the best way to produce a powerful feature is to load it with all the data first. Then, methodically chop, chop, chop until you've carved it into a sleek, precise piece of writing.

To demonstrate this, let's consider the story of the "Three Little Pigs," and discuss several conclusions we might draw from it.

========================

Once upon a time there were three little pigs who lived in a tiny house with their mother. They were a very happy family, but when the boys grew into full-sized oinkers, their mother had trouble feeding them.

She suggested it was time for them to leave the house and seek their fortunes. The three brothers—for reasons unknown except to the story's creator—don't share a dwelling. Instead, they wander off in opposite directions.

The first pig meets a man selling straw. He uses it to build an inexpensive, weak shack. A big wolf comes to the door and says, "Let me in, or I'll blow your house down."

When the pig refuses, Wolf puffs down the house, and Pig #1, who also neglected to buy homeowners' insurance, flees to join Pig #2.

Meanwhile, Pig #2 buys some sticks and constructs his abode with them. Mr. Wolf knocks on his door, makes the same threat, and follows through with that house-blowing-down thing again. Pigs #1 and #2 escape, squealing, to move in with their brother.

Pig #3, a realistic creature with some construction background, builds a substantial house of bricks. When Wolf assaults it, he hyperventilates while trying to blow it down. He then climbs onto the roof and attempts to enter the house through the chimney.

But Pig #3 places a pot of steaming water in the fireplace. When Wolf enters, he lands in that hot pot.

Wolf realizes that this is not a hog to be hounded, so he escapes, and never bothers the pigs again.

========================

Search for meaning

What important lessons does this story teach us?

1. Three pigs with no obvious means of support can save money sharing a house.
2. The cheapest product is not necessarily the best.
3. One should always plan an escape route from a dangerous situation.
4. It's important to prepare for a rainy day, or a wolf at the door, or an unexpected visitor for supper.
5. Every time you build a new means of entry (like a chimney), you must find a way to protect it.
6. Don't invite wolves and pigs to the same party.
7. Hope for the best, but prepare for the worst.

If you asked me, I'd say that items 2 and 7 were critical to this tale. You could build the story all sorts of ways—from the perspective of a pig or the wolf, for example—but the lessons are that (a) the cheapest isn't always the best, and (b) it's wise to prepare for the worst.

Now, recall Chapter 9. Let's put our list of first sentences to work for the "Three Little Pigs." For instance, let's plug in number 7, discovery, and see what happens.

"In the classic fairy tale 'Three Little Pigs,' we discover some important lessons about both quality and planning."

Now, let's move to number 24, What would you do? and see if we can make it fit.

"What would you do if you were one of the three little pigs, and a mean wolf was preparing to blow your house down?"

See how easy this is? If we select the what-would-you-do theme, we can follow with several more sentences and paragraphs within that framework. Additionally, if we take the role of Piggy #1 or #2, we can discuss how we escaped, plus our plans for future homebuilding.

Or we can bemoan our poor luck, but tell readers we've learned a lesson we can apply in the future, once again reinforcing the you-get-what-you-pay-for and prepare-for-the-worst themes.

The middle paragraphs: Declare and prepare

The toughest part of most short papers is the middle. How do you keep the reader engaged while constantly adding new information? Here's one idea.

Remember the cliffhanger technique, where we promise to reveal information later? *In the middle paragraphs, we declare, or provide information, in the first sentence, then prepare the reader for what's about to happen next with the second or third sentence.*

Let's rejoin the "Three Little Pigs" story:

=============================

What would you do if you were one of the three little pigs, and a mean wolf was preparing to blow your house down?

If you were the first pig, who built his house of straw, you'd suddenly realize the money you saved on construction is of no help now. (declare) And you'd also realize you needed to escape. But how? (prepare)

If you spent money on a front door, we hope you built a back one, too. (declare) It's always important to plan an escape route from danger. (declare) That way, you could escape to Pig #2's stick house, and see how he's doing. (prepare)

But Pig #2 also put economy ahead of safety, and built an inexpensive stick house. (declare) He's not in much better shape than you if the wolf comes calling. (declare) But Pig #3 could offer them both great advice. (prepare)

=============================

See how this little shortcut works? Each paragraph declares in the first part, and prepares (sets the stage) for the following paragraph at the end.

11
The ending...and how to begin it

I've always thought ending a story was like leaving a party. If I just grab my coat and walk out the door, people might wonder what happened. Was I upset? Was there an emergency?

Therefore, I must first prepare to leave by excusing myself from the conversation, thanking the hosts, and telling my friends goodbye. My exit, then, is part of a natural progression.

Likewise, ending a report or theme should sound natural to the reader. *If you begin the ending well, readers will expect the conclusion in the next few sentences.*

Following are 30 ways to say "so long," yet make the reader wish you'd stay. Oh yes, I've brought those three swine back into a few examples. Is this what they call pigging out?

1. *Headline reference.* (Suppose your headline, or title, reinforces the value of planning.) The three little pigs remind us that we can hope for the best, but we must prepare for the worst.

2. *Quote that restates the conclusion you've previously drawn.* No doubt Edgar Watson Howe was thinking of Pig #1 and Pig #2 when he said, "A good scare is worth more to a man than good advice."

3. *Discover*. The three pigs discovered that cutting corners and lack of preparation can be keys to disaster.

4. *Remember*. The pigs will always remember the two lessons they learned from the mean wolf.

5. *Success secrets*. The three pigs remind us that one secret to success is...

6. *Checklist*. Next time you find yourself in a dangerous predicament like our little pig friends, think about these three escape routes.

7. *Time constraint*. This story reminds us that home security systems can protect now, and warn against any wolves who come knocking tomorrow.

8. *Reinforce old saying*. That old saying "Here today, gone tomorrow" certainly describes the first two pigs' houses.

9. *Advice*. Follow the advice of Pig # 3, who told his brothers…

10. *Failed expectations*. The first two pigs never expected to find themselves homeless. They really needed homeowners' insurance.

11. *Numbering*. The pigs learned five things from their experience with the mean wolf.

12. *History lesson*. The pigs won't forget that day the wolf left them homeless, nor will they let this history repeat itself.

13. *Expert's advice*. David Lumber, an experienced builder, offers the pigs three reminders on future construction.

14. *Powerful evidence*. The pigs' experience offers convincing evidence that…

15. *Don't let this happen*. Don't let what happened to the three pigs happen to you.

16. *Shared traits*. Sometimes we humans, in an effort to save money and time, take the same path as the first two pigs.

17. *Inspirational thought*. In today's tough world, with wolves around every corner, it's nice to know that most of us still look after others.

18. *Writer's message*. I think about those three little pigs all the time, and how they supported each other. We'd do well to follow their example.

19. *Which one are you?* How do your classmates see you? As the friend who'll protect them from pain, or the wolf who tries to take advantage of each situation?

20. *Complete change*. Their brush with danger changed these three brothers from helpless piglets to independent hogs.

21. *What are the odds?* This story reminds us that 66% of homeowners don't carry enough insurance.

22. *Need more information?* Ever wonder if during hard times you could keep the wolf from your door? For an informative brochure, just call 000-000-0000.

23. *The facts are obvious*. We all know we must be prepared for the worst. We hear horror stories every day about unlocked homes. But what can we do about it today?

24. *Facts disprove theory*. So, despite the views of a few skeptics, Pig #3's actions prove that hogs can reason.

25. *Do me a favor*. If you believe as I do that pigs make good pets, write your congressman today and ask him to sponsor the Pork Barrel bill.

26. *Restated saying*. The pigs' well-fortified brick home not only kept the wolf away from the door, but discouraged his entry from the chimney, too.

27. *Want to read more?* For Three Pigs fans, two other excellent titles on the pig-and-wolf battles are...

28. *Luck or skill?* After all these years, readers can't decide. Did pure luck or good planning eventually save the pigs?

29. *Hidden meaning*. Sure, we can all learn a lesson about safety from the pigs. But the story's hidden meaning is this: A wolf who doesn't work out can't expect unlimited lung power when he needs it most.

30. *Topping a joke*. Sadly, the pigs discovered that the wolf's bark was worse than his bite, but his breath was the worst of all.

Five more ways to improve your writing

We're often asked why some stories get read, and others do not. Good question. But no definitive answer.

Problem is, writing's an art, not a science. But, since we've been around the block a few times—and been bitten by some vicious verbs—we've pulled together a few additional ideas.

1. Think about how you can present your idea in a fun way, if possible. (That's probably easier for the writer trying to sell products than it is for the student who must adhere to strict guidelines, or the researcher who must present a serious paper.)

2. Writing experts frequently argue about the value of humor. In fact, there's some research that claims folks read newspaper comics much more often than they do editorials.

No wonder! Most comics and cartoons (a) tell a brief story, (b) offer an upbeat conclusion, (c) focus on a single theme, and (d) teach without making value judgments. Can you make your writing do this?

3. Does contention help retention? In other words, should a writer talk negatively about an opposing position?

I don't think so. First, it's unseemly. Second, it requires additional evidence for proof or validation. Third, it diverts attention from the idea you are attempting to sell.

4. Groups of three -- Some people call them triads. These are *ideas presented in groups of three*, like "duty, honor, country," or "life, liberty, and the pursuit of happiness."

Even joke writers use this powerful form (There were these three guys who…). And so do fairy tales (Once upon a time there were three little pigs.)

Who knows what makes this a powerful literary device? Not I. But I use it often.

How can you? Well, how about this? Abe Lincoln's biography emphasizes hard work, creativity, and patriotism.

5. The purpose of short writing, I think, should be to get people interested enough to seek more information on a subject. It should encourage them to want to know more about you, and about your topic.

So, whenever I sit down to write words that stick, my main purpose is not to sell to someone, but simply to attract the reader to one simple premise.

12
Personal, inside information you should know

If you've stayed with *Words That Stick* this far, you're now holding a file folder full of ideas to help you craft short, powerful documents. The rest of this book contains a few personal observations, lessons learned through painful trial-and-error.

First, we'll look at reasons you should write from an expert perspective. And we'll show you how to get a reader's attention based on your specialty.

Has your writing ever been rejected? Sadly, it's a big part of school themes and writing competitions, and all writers must deal with it. I can't promise you'll learn to enjoy it, but perhaps there are some ways to repackage your work for better results.

Next, we'll discuss three more ways to make your writing rowboat stand out in a sea of battleships.

What's the most common form of quick correspondence today? E-mail, of course. So we'll pass along several tips on that, too.

Next, we'll briefly cover several types of media, and what kind of information each expects from you.

And, speaking of short writing, we'll add some thoughts on sales letters, short memos, and newsletters, too. Then, we'll answer some frequently asked questions about short writing.

In these first paragraphs on inside information, let's discuss the value of becoming an expert. In most fields, an expert on a particular subject is generally recognized as a valuable contributor, and is often sought out by the media.

How you can become an expert almost overnight

An expert is not some high-powered superhuman. An expert is simply a person who's well versed on a subject. All of us are experts on something.

I gained experience in short writing by talking to lots of editors, asking what they wanted and, more important, what they did not want.

Also, remember that the smaller your field, the fewer people will be found cultivating it. Here's an idea for narrowing your focus:

Let's say you know a lot about the theater. So do lots of other people. How can you separate yourself? How about focusing on only one type of show or time period, like early musicals?

To make the subject relevant to readers, you might relate the show's presentation to the present day. What tips can you offer current theater students from these long-ago performers?

Some painful thoughts on rejection

OK, you're off and running. You create a terrific news release. Then you craft a magnificent heading for it.

You send this wonderful work to an editor. Or, maybe you respond to a question about your profession in the newspaper, or you send out a direct mail solicitation.

You hear nothing. So you jump to the conclusion that no news is bad news. CONGRATULATIONS! YOU ARE RIGHT.

But cheer up! You've just taken a major step on that bumpy road to success. Because, you see, rejection is the first step to course correction. Course correction leads to better focus. Better focus leads to a clear picture of the goal and the road that takes you there.

Rejection can teach you three critical things:

1. You may need to alter your idea to fit the needs of your reader.

2. You may need to clarify your idea to help the reader or the editor understand it.

3. You may have presented your idea to the wrong editor or audience.

How to make your rowboat stand out in a sea of battleships

Unless you're a movie star, a politician, a radio/television celebrity, or all three, you'll have trouble getting the media to seek you out. That's because they mostly look for the bizarre, the unusual, or, in the case of politicians, both.

Therefore, if you hope to get published, or even noticed, it's helpful to know how to help the editor who can provide you with space.

We've said this before, but it's critical. *Surprise—in both the heading and lead paragraphs—is the best seller.* Make the reader say, "I must read more to see what happens next."

A great way to remind editors about what you do is to create an ongoing newsletter or sales letter. If it contains news or information, it could lead to a feature story about you.

Words That Stick tips for e-mail

It's a powerful communication tool, and one of the best places to make memorable comments.

This medium is so new, it's hard to find statistics on what types of messages folks read and save.

But thanks to Charlie Mouser of the Mouser Institute, and a few other experts, we've been able to compile a list of tips.

1. *Keep lines short.* Many experts advise keeping lines shorter than about 60 characters (that includes both letters and spaces), so they won't line-wrap.

2. *Headlines are critical.* Research reveals that when browsers look at material on the Internet, they check headlines before graphics.

3. *Write short copy.* I keep messages mighty short to encourage downloading by readers.

4. *Offer free information or details.* Personally, I've found this increases reader response.

5. *Don't use graphics*. I don't use them. Instead, I often make a point or separate thoughts with little signs on my keyboard like asterisks, the pound sign (#), and so on.

6. *Provide information before an advertisement*. I almost always give some sort of information before I propose an idea.

7. *Link to an e-mail address*. I personally prefer readers linking to my e-mail address instead of a Web site.

Reason? Recent research shows that only about 10% of readers who visit a Web site scroll past the first pages, and some may not sign the "guest book."

Alternative: Put a link to your Web site in your message, and ask readers to simply hit "Reply" and "Send" to get more details from you.

Several types of media, and what each one wants from you

I've sold stories to various publications for years. And I've also been rejected more often than a tone-deaf tenor at an opera audition. So, the following opinions are completely subjective. They're based on my personal experience working with and for the media.

1. *Neighborhood newsletters*. Many recipients are loyal readers, and the newsletters are usually hungry for news. If your targeted readers are local,

and you've got news to tell, this could be a great source. (Students, this could be a great place to get your first article published in addition to the school newspaper.)

2. *Shopper newspapers*. These are often weeklies, and may offer news coverage in addition to local ads. I've found that many of these papers use short filler features—about 25 to 100 words. Can you pitch your idea in this format?

3. *Weekly newspapers*. Most of these serve small towns or communities. Many are beautifully written and edited. Some will publish your news if it has relevance to that community, or is of a filler nature. This means it has no time immediacy, and is short enough to fit in a small space that opens up at the last minute.

4. *Semi-weeklies*. These generally serve mid-size towns, and are published twice a week. I love these papers, because they often have news holes to fit what I write.

5. *National trade magazines*. These are often monthlies, and serve a specific trade or profession. Almost every industry has one.

If you're an expert in a certain field or produce generic information that can apply to several fields (advertising, accounting, real estate, etc.), you could have great success offering articles to these editors.

This is my favorite medium, because I grew up the son of a trade magazine publisher, and have reported on several industries during my career.

6. *National trade newsletters*. These reach specific professional markets, much like trade magazines. And many are eager to publish anything of value to their readership.

7. *Local radio*. As you know, most radio stations target specific demographic audiences (teens, or males 35 to 60, or females, or sports fans). Also, the talk show market represents a terrific opportunity for you to be a guest, especially if you've got specific information to tell, and can promote it to radio show producers.

8. *National radio*. I used to produce a short humor spot, and place it as a filler feature. I suggest you approach radio stations with short pieces: 60-word (30 seconds), 120-word (one minute), or 240-word (two minute) stories.

9. *Daily newspapers*. These get huge readerships, but often have a large staff that gathers their own information. One way to approach them: Contact the "letters to the editor" section and respond to a news feature about your specialty with your additional comments on the subject.

Sales letters, short memos, and alternative approaches

Consider these popular sales letter approaches as your "transportation" to reach the reader, and to take the reader with you to the destination.

1. *Predictions*. You prognosticate a coming event, or predict a problem that might happen. Then, you come to the rescue by solving the anticipated problem.

2. *Testimonial letter*. This letter comes to you from a satisfied customer, complimenting your product or service. (I respond most quickly to this type of approach.)

Make sure you receive written permission from the customer or client to send this letter to other customers or clients.

3. *Secrets*. You offer to share with your reader a special secret about your expertise. Example: If you're a realtor, talk about the specific things you would look for before you buy yourself a new home.

A word about newsletters

There's not enough space here to discuss the benefits of newsletters as information tools. But we'll offer several reasons to start one.

Basic newsletters—perhaps just the front and back of a single sheet of paper—are inexpensive to print and distribute, yet often get great readership and response.

Newsletters are effective for neighborhood associations, civic groups, nonprofit organizations, or almost anyone who wants to reach a specific or special interest market.

For schools without funds to produce a school newspaper, a newsletter can be a good alternative for students to get work published.

(I've worked with several schools on approaches to newspaper publishing. One of the most helpful Web sites for them is www.my.highschooljournalism.org.)

E-mail newsletters are inexpensive to distribute and often get extremely quick responses. You must offer an easy way to "opt out," and include contact information (name, mailing address, telephone number, and e-mail address) in each one you send.

13
Answers to frequently-asked writing questions

This is the part where we attempt to answer anything that hasn't been covered so far.

Truth is, the only thing I know very much about is short writing. I've been doing it for years, and if forced to write a long essay I'd probably go crazy. So, that's why the answers that follow will be short…just like my attention span.

The stuff I've read so far makes sense, but I don't know how to begin. What do you suggest?

First, write down all the ways you can answer the teacher's requirement, or solve a reader's dilemma. Much nonfiction writing points out an obstacle, then offers a way to solve it. If you cannot state a problem clearly, then it's hard to propose a specific solution.

What common mistakes do you see in students' writing?

A major mistake is not sticking to *one single topic*. Often, a fine theme or research paper gets sidetracked because the writer starts in one direction, then suddenly shifts to another. Every paragraph should reinforce and expand on the central theme.

Another mistake is stilted writing. Very few of us write like we talk, yet that's a great skill. *One*

way to improve your paper: Read it out loud.
You'll quickly hear where the wording sounds too fancy, stiff, or unnatural.

One of the most "pressurized" writing assignments any student faces is the personal essay for college applications. I am absolutely NOT an expert here, but I'll be glad to share a few thoughts. Although each school requires a unique focus, you may, in general, want to:

1. Consider this a chance to elaborate on your unique experiences, special skills, or success experiences.

2. Remember that the person who reads your essay has read hundreds of others already. Think of what you can say in the first couple of sentences to make her think, "Wow, what a great idea."

3. Should the essay be erudite or amusing? That's not for me to say. But, here's one thought: *Can you tell a personal story in a way that reveals a universal truth?* For example, think again how Tom Sawyer's fence-painting episode reminds readers that work can be fun if presented right.

Do you mean "revealing a universal truth" by telling a story?

We readers absorb information best if it's placed in STORY context. Go back to Chapter 4, and look at the six elements of a biographical essay.

As you'll remember from classic tales like "The Tortoise and the Hare" and "Little Red Riding Hood," memorable stories often pair the *character* with the *problem* he or she must overcome. Every main character needs a mountain to climb, or a problem to solve!

I don't have any training as a writer.

So what? You don't need a degree to make an impression. Mark Twain completed only three years of formal schooling, and Abraham Lincoln about one. Yet they became lifelong learners, and darn fine writers too.

I have a very small budget for marketing and public relations. Any alternatives?

Do you have customer and prospect e-mail addresses? If so, e-mail your news message to them.

What's the best way to close my message, and implant those "words that stick"?

Many people say it's to offer the reader several ways to get free additional information (toll-free phone number, Web site, e-mail address, fax).

Is there a fast-growing specialty in the media business?

There appears to be a great demand for explainers in every industry. *These are industry experts who put technical details in layman's terms.* Could you do this for your industry?

What makes people remember things better?

Memory experts tell us we must implant ideas. One way is through repetition. Another way is to appeal to as many senses as possible (seeing, hearing, touching, smelling, tasting).

My wife, a former teacher, said she would often present new information to students, then call on them immediately to get them to repeat that information to her.

And of course, if you deliver the information orally, you can encourage the listeners to write it down. That's another way to help them implant the idea in their brains.

Memory, we're told, is both short-term and long-term. We must hold a person's interest long enough for her to transfer it from the short-term to the long-term memory.

Do we 21st century humans suffer from receiving too much information?

New research on attention spans offers frightening results. Apparently, the more messages we're exposed to, the less attention we pay to each one.

One theory claims we have selective focus, and screen out anything that's not of immediate interest. Another assumption is that there's so much information around, we just can't absorb it all.

What's the typical focus length? Some say it's a measly eight seconds. So, I'll say it again. Shorten the message and simplify the focus.

***What if I've got a "hostile audience," a group
who will disagree with what I've got to say?***

Politicians deal with this all the time! They
often start a speech by talking about common
problems, like how to educate our children better
or save for our retirement years. If we start with
common, shared goals, perhaps readers will be
more willing to follow our thoughts when we lead
them down new pathways, too.

Strange, but it's said that the less we know
about a candidate, the more we like him! (Think
about this during the next election.) Why?

Perhaps it's because the more he's forced to
reveal, the more specific he must be, and the more
likely he is to offend one group or another.

*In these pages, we've talked repeatedly about
brief messages.*

*Why do people expend so much effort writing
detailed, complicated copy if nobody reads it,
keeps it, refers to it, or remembers it? Why-oh-why
do we want to stay with our readers so darn long
when they'll like us more if we just give 'em
something to smile or think about, then leave?*

*The shorter the prose, the longer we seem to
remember it. Example: Lincoln's Gettysburg
Address.*

*I'm told that present-day politicians often try to
reduce messages to short, one-or-two-sentence
"sound bites." They try to say something short
and memorable, something profound enough to
earn a mention on a news program!*

But what if my idea's not hot news?

Watch the newspaper for anything that pertains to your field. When the article appears, write a letter to the editor about it, referencing when the story appeared, and give the reason you're writing.

For example: "I saw your April 3 article on spring cleaning. Because my company cleans offices professionally, I wanted to share these additional tips with your readers."

Editors might keep your name and phone number, so they can call you for background information whenever additional news on that subject appears.

14
22 sample documents that use Words That Stick

Here comes my favorite part of this book, next to my name on the front cover. (It's still there, right?)

We'll show you samples of several letters, short reports, and themes that apply Words That Stick glue.

You'll note that some don't need a heading, because they're personal correspondence. Also, in each sample we'll use a captivating first-sentence example from Chapter 9, which we'll list by number in parentheses next to the sentence.

So, in each case, go back to Chapter 9 to see which one(s) we used.

Some people insist that a paragraph should express a complete thought and stand alone. However, to communicate a single idea to the reader through a series of paragraphs, each one should link to the paragraph before it. Would you like a trick to help you remember this?

Then think of your work as a long locomotive. The powerful engine (the first sentence or two) pulls every other car on the train because each is linked to the one before it. Most large trains also have a caboose, a car most people recognize as the end of the long series of boxcars, trailer cars, and tanker cars.

> *You must have a powerful beginning, links that tie each paragraph to the one before it, and a distinctive ending to reinforce the theme.*
>
> *Does this make sense? If so, consider yourself officially "trained."*

Also, even in short, informal letters, keep in mind the declare-and-prepare idea we discussed in Chapter Ten. In every case, we want to convince the reader that the material is worth reading, lead the reader in a logical, linear process, and offer a satisfying, memorable conclusion.

1. Thank-you note

Dear Mrs. Teacher,

I'll always remember the first day I walked into your class, and how your wonderful lectures always motivated me to strive for truth and accuracy. (# 9)

So I hope you realize how very much your congratulation note meant to me. In fact, I plan to frame it along with my high school diploma, because your encouragement kept me moving forward...

2. Congratulations

Dear Ron,

I've always known that your quick thinking and problem-solving skills would take you a long way. (# 55) So you can imagine how proud I am to be a friend of the new congressman from this district!

3. Announcement

Dear friends,

Who says, "You can't teach an old dog new tricks"? (# 20)

I'm proud to tell you that my husband Bob just completed a marathon without collapsing! That's amazing, considering his training routine.

4. Condolence

Dear Mary,

We still cannot believe that your remarkable husband Steve is no longer with us. Those of us who worked with him considered him a living legend in our industry. (# 26 and # 49)

5. Obituary or funeral oration

Our friend David lived a modest life, and if he were sitting with us today he'd be embarrassed by all this attention! But, many of us are here to say thank you to this humble man who anonymously gave away thousands of dollars to help deserving students complete their educations. (# 25)

David, as most of you know, paid his entire way through school working nights at the newspaper. (# 29) What's even more impressive is the struggle David endured just to get to work each evening. (# 44)

Later in life, when David began to realize his dreams, (# 46) he vowed to help others do the same.

6. Invitation

Please join us March 25 to celebrate Larry's 45th birthday with a "hidden treasure" party. What's a "hidden treasure" party?
(# 54)

We'll each come to the event, and share a reason why we consider Larry to be a treasure to this community.

7. Letter to family member

Dear kid sister Sarah,

Because you're so much younger, I always considered us completely different personalities. But today, as we gather at Mom and Dad's house to celebrate your 21st birthday, I believe we're very much alike. (# 3 and # 50)

8. Cover letter for resume

Dear Ms._____:

There's a new category of customer for your research books. I found these customers on my college campus last year. (# 52)

As a history and statistics major who works in the university bookstore, I spend lots of time talking to shoppers. I was extremely curious why students bought books not specifically required for classes.

Here's what they told me: *(In the next couple of paragraphs, the applicant details the research.)*

Ms. _____, I hope you will be able to use this data, and also consider me for your research assistant position. But to do so, I'm sure you'll need more information about my background and skills. On the next page you'll find my resume. There's much more I'd like to know about your company. When would be a convenient time for me to meet with you?

9. Letter of introduction (or recommendation)
Dear Mr. _____:

I want to introduce you to a young lady who grew up next door to me. I never realized how special she was until one day last summer, when her quick thinking and college training saved a life. (# 54 and # 8)

This special person, Debbie _____, graduated from nursing school last month. She has been working part-time in our hardware store while sending resumes to hospitals.

Last week, an older gentleman collapsed at our store. *(Briefly tell the rest of the story.)*

Debbie has specialized training, a cool head in the midst of chaos, and a sincere desire to help others. I think she'd make a valuable addition to your staff.

10. Office memo
Heading: New information (# 4)
Good morning, Bob,

I thought you'd like to see the test results on our Model 305 widget, which shows it lasts nearly twice as long as the old model. Why?

According to this report from the field, the 305's material simply performs better under extreme conditions. But perhaps you should read the details below before we talk to the folks in marketing.

11. Client memo
Heading: Predictions for winter sales (# 10 and # 19)

Hello, Tom,

None of us really knows what's going to happen this winter. But according to the latest long-term weather forecasts—which I've detailed below—you'll want to stock up on snow tires.

Here are three reasons why right now is a good time to buy... (# 14)

12. Confirmation
Hello, Sam,

What a great surprise to find out you received our order last night, and shipped the inventory items this morning! (# 54)

All of us at this store appreciate your special ability to anticipate our needs, and deliver items so promptly and courteously. (# 55)

13. Rejection
Dear Mr. _____:

Thank you for applying for the regional territory manager position. Although that specific job has been filled, there may still be an opportunity for you in local sales. (# 41)

14. Complaint
Dear Mr. _____:

My uncle used to tell me "a company can't fix a problem if the customer doesn't say something about it." (# 42)

So, let me tell you about a situation in one of your stores last week, and how—working together—we might solve it to everyone's satisfaction. (# 43)

15. Fundraising
Heading: For 10 years we've helped others, and now they're helping us. (# 13)

A decade ago, Steve _____ was one of the first clients we served. Having just arrived in our town, Steve needed a place to stay and a warm meal. We helped him…and now he's paying us back in a big way.

Steve works one evening a week here at the Community Food Bank. "That night ten years ago turned my life around," he told us. How did we help Steve?

16. New product press release
Heading: New CD offers shortcut to memorization (# 15)

Most of us want to read faster and retain more. (# 2) In the next three paragraphs we'll show you three shortcuts to quick learning. (# 15)

17. News release
Heading: Fitness expert reveals new discovery (# 7)

"Many people," claims fitness expert John Pushup, "start a workout program, but quit in just a few weeks because the routine becomes monotonous." (# 18 and # 37) However, John suggests a new alternative.

18. Letter to the editor

Dear Editor:

Your paper's June 25 story on the city's plan to dramatically change our traditional July 4th parade shocked and surprised me. (# 11)

Have you considered that attendance might drop significantly if the parade gets moved from its central downtown location?

From previous news reports, I recall that the typical spectator now travels only three miles to see the parade. The new location forces the typical spectator to travel seven miles.

19. Sales letter

Heading: Why do so many business people forget this one simple idea? (# 6)

Sales trainer Tom _____ insists the two-word, courteous "thank you" can be said in many ways. (# 2) Here are five ways to tell your customer how much you appreciate her. (# 12)

Here are three ways you can simplify messages, starting TODAY:

1. SINGLE PAGE LIMIT -- When you write a letter, memo, or e-mail, try to hold it to 250 words or less. Everybody is busy, busy, busy. But most folks can make time to examine one page.

*2. REINFORCE A SINGLE THEME—Your
headline or first sentence should make a powerful
statement. Everything else in the memo or letter
should reinforce that.*

*3. BUSINESS CARD SLOGAN -- Could you
explain your major theme in two lines beneath
your name on a business card? Think about the
prime benefit you offer and the reason people
should agree with your idea.*

20. Political speech

When people tell me they grew up poor, I can
empathize, because I wasn't born with a silver
spoon in my mouth. (# 29) But the best thing
about this country is that we can start poor, and
still create the kind of life we want. (# 46) Today
I'd like to tell you about my five-step plan to make
this country even better. (# 28)

(If you read Chapter 9 again, you'll note that
almost every way to begin a story can be worked
into a political speech. Amazing!)

21. Mini-biography or personality profile

Heading: Unforgettable teacher changes many
lives (# 9)

Each spring Mrs. Irma Instructor, 75, bids
another tearful class of graduating seniors
goodbye. (# 13) Many of them realize her
compassion and communication skills taught them
lessons they'll never forget. (# 42)

What are the secrets of her teaching method? (#
55) And what continues to motivate this

remarkable woman who works, in her words, "for the joy of watching students learn"? (# 25)

22. Research report

Heading: Field tests indicate consumer demand (# 23 in Chapter Six)

If field reports are any indication, retailers are responding well to our new "how-to" video on the Model 773. (# 1)

Retailer Terry Inventory, the nation's leading dealer for the 773, says, "Customers tell us the video helps them put the 773 to work immediately." (# 37 and # 38)

Epilogue

The most important light in our house is the smallest one. Like many other families, we keep a tiny nightlight in a dark hallway.

That bulb's kept me safe for years. When our child was little, it illuminated a path to her room, so we wouldn't stumble if she called us. Later, it kept us from tripping over our large and frequently sleeping dog.

Not long ago, before guests came over, I pulled the light out so I could plug in a vacuum cleaner. Then I forgot where I had put it.

Bad idea! We couldn't find the nightlight for several days, and I stumbled around in the dark.

It's a wonderful product. Its simple mission is clear, and it brightens the area that needs it most.

Your words can do the same thing. Focused, short messages can glow forever. Powerful, simple passages are much like that little bulb, illuminating and inspiring others.

Words that stick. Words that live forever. Words that glow.

In this little book, we've provided a few designs to help you build bright, illuminated paragraphs. But it's your own thoughts, enthusiasm, and creativity that will supply the spark.

Acknowledgments

I appreciate Doris Norvelle-Briscoe, head of English/ Language Arts for the Fort Worth Independent School District, who first gave me the opportunity to create workshops for journalism teachers.

On the state level, I thank Brenda Ellis of the Region 8 Education Service Center for allowing me to present programs for teachers in the East Texas area.

I also appreciate the kind reviews for this book following the release of the First Edition in 2004. This newly-revised Second Edition addresses some additional questions, and – I hope – provides new and relevant answers.

Finally, a long-overdue thanks to Mrs. Winifred Elliott, my English teacher at Fort Worth's Paschal High School, who set high writing standards and constantly encouraged me to do my best.

CPSIA information can be obtained at www.ICGtesting.com
Printed in the USA
LVOW061825160911

246663LV00001B/4/P

9 781602 648739